IT'S TIME TO EAT GREEN HUMMUS

It's Time to Eat GREEN HUMMUS

Walter the Educator

Silent King Books
A WhichHead Entertainment Imprint

Copyright © 2025 by Walter the Educator

All rights reserved. No part of this book may be reproduced in any manner whatsoever without written per- mission except in the case of brief quotations embodied in critical articles and reviews.

First Printing, 2024

Disclaimer

This book is a literary work; the story is not about specific persons, locations, situations, and/or circumstances unless mentioned in a historical context. Any resemblance to real persons, locations, situations, and/or circumstances is coincidental. This book is for entertainment and informational purposes only. The author and publisher offer this information without warranties expressed or implied. No matter the grounds, neither the author nor the publisher will be accountable for any losses, injuries, or other damages caused by the reader's use of this book. The use of this book acknowledges an understanding and acceptance of this disclaimer.

It's Time to Eat GREEN HUMMUS is a collectible early learning book by Walter the Educator suitable for all ages belonging to Walter the Educator's Time to Eat Book Series. Collect more books at WaltertheEducator.com

USE THE EXTRA SPACE TO TAKE NOTES AND DOCUMENT YOUR MEMORIES

GREEN HUMMUS

It's time to eat, hooray, hooray!

It's Time to Eat Green Hummus

A yummy snack is on its way.

It's smooth and creamy, green and bright,

A tasty treat, oh, what a sight!

We call it hummus, soft and spread,

Made with chickpeas, nice and red.

A little garlic, lemon too,

And something green, can you guess who?

Spinach, parsley, maybe peas,

Blend them up with such great ease!

They make our hummus fresh and fun,

A healthy bite for everyone!

Dip a cracker, take a taste,

Not a single bit will waste.

Crunch and munch, so soft inside,

A snack that fills our hearts with pride!

It's Time to Eat Green Hummus

Try it with some carrot sticks,

Or celery for crunchy kicks!

Spread it on some warm, soft bread,

A happy tummy lies ahead!

Green hummus helps us grow so strong,

It makes our bodies sing along!

Protein, vitamins, so good,

It gives us super eating mood!

Mom and Dad both take a bite,

They smile and say, "Oh, what delight!"

Even Grandma claps her hands,

Green hummus is her favorite brand!

Brother says, "I'll give it try,"

He dips his chip and says, "Oh my!"

"It's really yummy, I agree!

It's Time to Eat Green Hummus

Pass the bowl and share with me!"

So next time when it's time to eat,

Try green hummus, such a treat!

Healthy, tasty, smooth, and fun,

Snack time joy for everyone!

Now our tummies feel just right,

Full of goodness, pure delight.

Thank you, hummus, green and bright,

It's Time to Eat Green Hummus

For making snack time feel so right!

ABOUT THE CREATOR

Walter the Educator is one of the pseudonyms for Walter Anderson. Formally educated in Chemistry, Business, and Education, he is an educator, an author, a diverse entrepreneur, and he is the son of a disabled war veteran. "Walter the Educator" shares his time between educating and creating. He holds interests and owns several creative projects that entertain, enlighten, enhance, and educate, hoping to inspire and motivate you. Follow, find new works, and stay up to date with Walter the Educator™

at WaltertheEducator.com

www.ingramcontent.com/pod-product-compliance
Lightning Source LLC
LaVergne TN
LVHW052012060526
838201LV00059B/3994